PERSONAS *With* PUNCH

TRUE STORIES OF SIX PERSONAS THAT MADE A DIFFERENCE FOR MARKETERS, COMPANIES, AND THEIR BOTTOM LINE

by
Wayne Cerullo

with
Dennis Flynn
Scott Hornstein

CONTENTS

OVERVIEW

In the last few years, "buyer personas" have become a standard marketing tool or concept.

A recent B2P industry survey, The Power and Potential of Personas, showed that over half of B2B marketers (63%) are using personas and another one-quarter (24%) say they will start using personas in the next 1-2 years. According to Boardview, 83% of B2B marketers plan to be using personas in the near future. B2P conducts and publishes this research annually.

WHAT IS THE IMPACT OF PERSONAS?

But now that it's standard for any competent marketer to use personas, we face the next two questions:

- **Are those personas any good?** By that we mean, do they actually tell us anything we <u>didn't already know</u>, or are they just <u>summaries of the obvious</u>?

- **Do those personas help us go to market any better?** Do they improve our targeting, differentiation, message delivery, message response, prospect conversion, or shorten the sales cycle?

In other words,

Do personas really matter?

YES... AND NO

The answer, of course, is... it depends. The purpose of this e-book is to equip and encourage you with real-life examples of when the answer has been **yes**.

There does appear to be hope that personas can make a difference.

- According to Boardview, fully 71% of companies who exceed revenue and lead goals have documented personas.

- BrightTALK adds that using buyer personas as a basis in email campaigns doubles the open rate and increases click through by 500%.

- Finally, HubSpot finds that using buyer personas makes a website 2x – 5x easier to use for targeted users.

On the other hand, there is ample evidence that MANY personas are NOT making a difference. From our research:

- 63% of marketers surveyed report that personas are only somewhat effective.

- 35% cite a major frustration that personas are not respected by others in the organization.

WHAT CAN PERSONAS TEACH US?

Having created many, many personas over the years, we have seen what goes into making them more or less valuable.

There are three kinds of learning that emerge from persona work.

1. **What you didn't know you didn't know.** This is the most powerful source of insights. It emerges from our open-ended exploration of how your prospects go about solving the problem for which your product is the solution.

2. **Correction of what you thought incorrectly.** This could be to change an idea or to reset the importance of a perception. For example, you may have thought that having a particular need was a defining characteristic of your prospect, only to uncover that their personal beliefs about how to address that need are far more important.

3. **Confirmation of what you know.** While this seems to have little benefit, it actually does help to hear – in their own words – how prospects think about their situation and your potential solution. In particular, we help you focus on what is most important among the myriad things you know about your prospect. And perhaps most importantly, it identifies a positive point of connection among various internal groups who share a common understanding of who you are working together to serve.

WHAT'S YOUR POINT?

All personas describe the person they profile. But a description can have infinite facets. The same person who is a "soccer mom" can also be a senior financial officer or a health food fanatic... it depends on what aspects of their person your persona references.

Key Prospect Insight is the key truth that connects your prospects with your product.

Some personas go in the wrong direction by including interesting aspects of their personality (for example, that a financial officer who is also a health food fanatic) that are nonetheless irrelevant and distracting.

We believe it is a best practice for personas to be focused rather than scattered, and take you to a point [Shabbir - bold that word], not just to a person. We call this point the Key Prospect Insight [Shabbir - bold that phrase]. It is the key truth that holds the power to connect your prospect with your product or service.

Identifying the Key Prospect Insight is the core reason we create personas -- to uncover how they might be engaged with a client's offering, not to "dress up" a profile with colorful descriptions of the meals and movies they like.

WHY 'PROSPECT' PERSONAS?

By this point, you have likely heard people refer to "personas" in several different ways. This may reflect that they are actually referring to different kinds of personas.

- **"User personas"** were developed by Alan Cooper in the 1980's as a way to guide early software development that could be used by business people who were not trained as computer scientists. This was introduced as a planning tool in The Inmates are Running the Asylum in 1998.

- **"Buyer personas"** were a natural evolution to the marketing world that occurred a few years later. Especially in the B2B world, these personas were helpful for product marketers to focus on how and why business people might consider buying a product, not just the product features.

- **"Prospect personas"** are a further development of the concept to account for the increasing size of the B2B buying team and complexity of the B2B buying process.

- For example, the CEB estimates that an average of 5.4 individuals are actively involved with a typical B2B purchase decision, and many more are involved if the purchase is large or strategic.

- B2P introduced this concept to account for the fact that many of those involved are not "buyers" but nonetheless are very important "influencers", "researchers", or "gatekeepers".

- In addition, the growth of SaaS and cloud services means that "your" customers may also be your competitor's customers. And even your most loyal customers are only a click away from selecting an online alternative.

- As a result, we favor thinking of all external stakeholders as "prospects". It's not only more realistic – it's wiser!

- **"Account personas"** are the final variation we have developed on this theme, reflecting that teams of purchasers in "decision-making units" vary from one another, depending on their industry, need, and even individual companies. You do not sell to Exxon the same way you sell to WeWork or the Defense Department, even if you are selling the same goods to all. This is beyond the scope of this book, but you ought to be aware of the concept.

MARKETING SITUATIONS / OBJECTIVES

We have applied Prospect Personas to improve the impact of ongoing marketing efforts as well as to prepare marketers to enter markets that are new or evolving. We have applied them to these eight specific scenarios.

6

Increasing your market impact:

1. **Marketing Effectiveness** – to increase the impact of the marketing you are already doing through better targeting, messaging, and differentiation.

2. **Purchase Cycle Acceleration** – to simplify and speed your sales cycle by better aligning your sales process with your prospects' buying process.

3. **Differentiation** – to increase and sharpen communication of the points of differenentiation most important to your prospects.

4. **Sales Engagement** – to better equip the sales team with insights about who to target and how to help them buy more effectively.

Expansion / evolution:

5. **Market Introduction** – for the effective launch of a new product or disruptive technology.

6. **Market Expansion** – for an existing product entering a new market.

7. **Market Evolution** – for an existing product competing in a market changed by a new technology, competitor, or buying process.

8. **Vertical Marketing** – for an existing product looking to penetrate a particular industry more effectively.

PERSONA EXAMPLES

All this is just nice theory without real-life examples of personas in action. That is why we have gathered a half-dozen examples of personas we have created that have made a big difference in the life of the companies that commissioned them.

Each of these companies thought they **already knew a lot** about their product and their markets **before** they decided to invest in understanding their prospects better – and still:

- each one **discovered new insights** about their prospects

- that made an **important difference** in the way they managed their go-to-market strategy, marketing communications, sales efforts, and marketing budget

- and **improved their sales, profitability, and market presence**

- from the **same resources** they otherwise would have spent less productively.

Each would claim to have reaped a high **"return on insight"** (a particular kind of ROI) from their investment of time and money to understand their prospects and the prospect journey.

In fact, the goal of all persona development work is to create a **competitive marketing advantage** for the company that leverages its superior understanding of who are the best prospects, what those prospects most want, why they might favor that offering, and how they go through the purchase process.

Accordingly, to protect their confidentiality, we have not identified the clients in these cases (with two obvious exceptions). Included are stories from a wide range of companies and industries:

- Some of the **largest multinationals** on the planet for whom not succeeding was unacceptable.

- Some **remarkably small companies** who really wanted to get the most impact from their limited resources.

- Some **mid-tier companies** looking to compete smarter against large competitors with greater resources.

- Some **huge but stagnant** markets along with some **small, fast-growth** industries.

THE SIX PERSONAS WITH IMPACT

These six initial persona examples reflect a range of B2B categories, including hardware (commercial energy storage devices and hospital pump systems) as well as software as a service (SaaS) offerings, such as data security and data backup.

Company sizes vary from two Fortune 500 firms to several startups and even a consulting firm with fewer than a dozen professionals but national ambitions.

The B2B industries reflected in these stories vary from engineering to business services to healthcare to information technology.

- **Data backup service** – a story about market expansion and competitive differentiation.

- **Hospital IV pump system** – a story about marketing effectiveness, marketing evolution, and competitive differentiation.

- **Business merchandising services for SMB** – a story about market evolution, a new market introduction, and competitive differentiation.

- **Backup energy technology** – a story about market introduction, market expansion, and vertical marketing.

- **Data security SaaS** – a story about market introduction, marketing effectiveness and purchase cycle acceleration.

- **Environmental consulting** – a story about marketing effectiveness and purchase cycle acceleration.

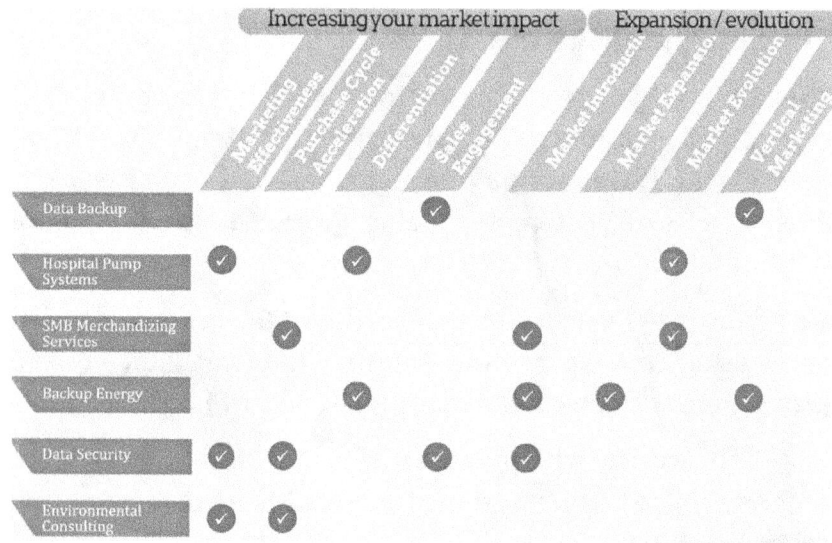

HOW THEY DID IT

One small, but important point about this story... notice that the impact on the business came not from simply "doing" a persona, but from **how** they did it.

- They conducted **real research** with **real prospects** – they did not sit in a conference room and "make up" a persona from their assumptions.

- They explored how prospects thought in an **open-ended** manner – they did not survey pre-identified questions on how many people said X or Y.

- They made sure to understand the **context and process** for buying any security software, not just what they liked about this version.

- They **challenged their assumptions** – even though they seemed well-founded – and applied **new learning** to yield **new outcomes**.

OK – now let's find out what they found out... and what difference it made.

PERSONA
Story 1

WHAT YOU DON'T
KNOW CAN KILL YOU!

A story about market expansion and competitive differentiation for a small data backup software company taking on some of the largest competitors on Earth.

Our story begins with a talented, young software engineer, named David Farajun, working days and nights to complete a mission-critical program for his employer. He was nearly done. Days away from completion. And then... nothing.

The computer system burped, and all the data was lost, instantly. Just as quickly, the company was out of business, and David was out of a job.

OUT OF BUSINESS BUT NOT OUT OF IDEAS

But not out of ideas. In response, he decided to pivot and began developing the best backup program he could imagine and created a business backing up everyone else's data.

14

The company David started, Asigra, is one of the most dynamic organizations you've never heard of, quietly providing data backup and recovery services to small and medium-sized businesses (SMB) through channel partners. They serve more than a half million sites throughout the world, over all business sectors.

Their record of innovations is impressive for such a small company. As the first company to put backup and recovery in the cloud, their tag line appropriately and proudly was "The Cloud Backup Experts."

Scrolling ahead to the present day, recent developmental "firsts" caused Asigra's software to be included by industry analysts among preferred enterprise-grade backup solutions. This was more than analysis or publicity, this was an expert endorsement that they were ready to move to the enterprise.

But it became frustrating for everyone to find that having a superior offering did not automatically open opportunities.

In fact, it was draining their resources and morale. They needed to find a way to attract attention and create credibility against the likes of Symantec, IBM, and Commvault. These companies had long and wide-ranging relationships throughout enterprise IT staff, based on having a wide range of offerings, one of which was data backup.

And to make matters worse, these 500 lb. gorillas of data management were so massive they could simply give away data backup as a free service. Breaking in was going to be very hard.

GOING TO THE SOURCE

The good news in all this bad news was that it was really clear that the company needed to compete smarter, not just harder. They decided that the only way they were going to succeed was if they could approach the market in a way no one else was. And they had only one opportunity to get it right.

It became clear that getting to the CIO and the specific data manager was essential to determining a successful direction. As a result, they decided to go to the source – the enterprise individuals whose minds they had to change.

Asigra needed a deep understanding of what it was doing wrong and what it could do right. How do these decision makers they see the weaknesses of the competition and the strengths of Asigra? How do these decision makers express their needs?

Asigra decided to create "Prospect Personas" to better understand these enterprise IT decision makers as people, with intertwining, and sometimes contradictory, personal and professional goals, needs and preferences, to understand how they make decisions.

These personas were composite representations of their prospects, based on in-depth, open-ended exploratory conversations with real target prospects. In this case, they were enterprise IT decision makers who were asked about their attitudes regarding backup and recovery processes and technologies, including their company's expectations, their day-to-day challenges, emerging technologies, and how they learn (or don't).

It would not have been unusual for the company to reject doing this kind of "soft" prospect research since:

- They had practically invented the product category
- They had decades of experience in it
- It was a technical product sold to technical buyers by a technical sales force
- They had limited resources for marketing

But then, they would not have discovered any of these buying insights...

FOUR BUYING CHALLENGES

Asigra had to address four challenges if they were to realize their enterprise aspirations:

- Data backup was not seen as strategic, but as a pain in the butt — a low-level, cost-centric, time-intensive process. Just getting a meeting to discuss the topic was a major effort. Calling a company "the cloud backup experts" was exactly the wrong way to get into the enterprise.

- These senior IT executives were responsible to their corporation for how quickly, efficiently, and completely data can be recovered.

    "Recoverability is the goal. If something goes wrong, how easy is it to get your data back. Nothing else matters"

- At this time, many enterprise decision makers had an almost religious aversion to cloud backup and recovery and would stop paying attention once it was mentioned. Which meant that Asigra was positioning themselves in <u>exactly</u> the wrong way ("the cloud backup experts") to get into the enterprise.

  "Many of us in security have an illogical distrust of the cloud. I can't touch my data. It's emotional."

- Finally, enterprise decision makers were not about to trust their critical data to a company they never heard of. As one of them commented:

  "I didn't get into the security business because I trust people."

POSITIONING FOR WHAT PROSPECTS WANT

These insights led to a complete reconsideration of Asigra's positioning for the enterprise marketplace. Asigra rallied around a new mantra, a new flag, a new single-minded focus of strategic importance, "Recovery is Everything." This aligned themselves with the real concerns of the enterprise IT leaders and was disruptive in a marketplace that messaged backup. The cloud, which one IT director said "blocks out the sun" for him, was relegated to an unstated feature.

All communications were redesigned, from the web, to email, to the signage in their corporate offices. A new logo signaled the change to employees and channel partners. Additional enterprise-level channel partners were attracted and signed up. And a new advertising campaign announced the new positioning to the industry.

When something's missing, everything's wrong.

FIRE

BREAK GLASS
USE HAMMER

When it comes to recovering your data, there's no such thing as a minor detail.

Good thing there's Asigra. Our award-winning recovery solution lets you recover now from anywhere. Every byte. Any device. All the time. How can we make such a promise? Because we've been leading the recovery revolution for more than 25 years— with more than a million installations worldwide.

Find out more today at recoveryiseverything.com. And never be burned by a data loss again.

Asigra.
Recovery is Everything

www.asigra.com

19

<u>But wait... there's more</u>

Asigra's Vice President of Marketing summarized their new prospect-centered positioning:

"The Prospect Persona methodology gave us the positioning we needed to highlight our strength and distance ourselves from the formidable competition. As a result, we are messaging Disaster Recovery as a Service and data protection. It really IS all about the 'recovery' – business continuity and disaster recovery."

Asigra was so focused and enthusiastic about this new positioning that they refocused their pricing model on data recovery rather than data backup. Where all competitors were charging for the tonnage of data stored, Asigra offered an alternative - to charge by the amount of data recovered, which is typically 10% - 15% of the data stored. Now customers could align their expenditures with the ultimate value to the corporation and reduce budgetary demands at the same time.

THE POWER OF PROSPECT-CENTERED POSITIONING

As Asigra brought this new positioning to market, they initially experienced over a 15% increase in unique visitors to their website. Then, they began to get invited to respond to RFPs from large education, manufacturing, and automotive companies. They also found great interest among government agencies with high security requirements.

Conversations with the private sector revealed that disaster recovery was synonymous with business continuity. Two years into their enterprise push, Tech Target named them the top enterprise backup and recovery software, and did so again the next year, over Commvault, Symantec, HP, and IBM.

Beyond the marketplace response, it was gratifying to hear David, the founder, respond to the new description of his life's work:

"Those three words
– 'Recovery is Everything' –
capture all that I have been working
on for all these years."

About the Author

International author, lecturer, and consultant, Scott Hornstein has worked with clients in all phases of marketing strategy, research, and implementation. His customer relationship methodology emphasizes respect and trust, and promotes opt-in relationships between marketers and their customers to maximize customer satisfaction, retention, and lifetime value.

He has worked with companies large and small to introduce and build new ideas to profitability, implement high-quality lead programs, improve marketing performance and accountability, and reengineer customer interfaces to boost satisfaction, referral, and return on investment.

B2B clients who have benefited from Scott's expertise include Microsoft, IBM, HP, AT&T, and Merrill Lynch, as well as Viryd Technologies, Applied Biosystems, Franklin Covey, and PaperDirect.

Scott's most recent book is <u>Opt-In Marketing</u>, and a second book will be coming out later this year. His articles and interviews have appeared in Brandweek, Adweek, Sales & Marketing Management, CRM, Catalog Age, BtoB, DMA Insider, The Toronto Star, and more. Scott's ability to make client companies hum reflects his own penchant for jazz, playing in an ensemble near his home base in Redding, CT.

PERSONA
Story 2

WORST TO FIRST BY
LEARNING FROM OTHERS

A story about marketing effectiveness, marketing evolution, and competitive differentiation for a hospital IV pump manufacturer needing to recover years of lost ground to capable competitors.

There's nothing quite so dangerous as success. At one time, this company was the pre-eminent manufacturer and supplier of hospital IV pumps.

NEVER WASTE A GOOD CRISIS

Then, one day, they woke up to find that a new technology had been introduced, and it was eating their lunch. To make matters worse, the FDA objected to some of their software testing protocols and demanded that they replace or remediate all existing pumps. It was a one-two punch that would have put all but the most resilient and agile corporations down for the count.

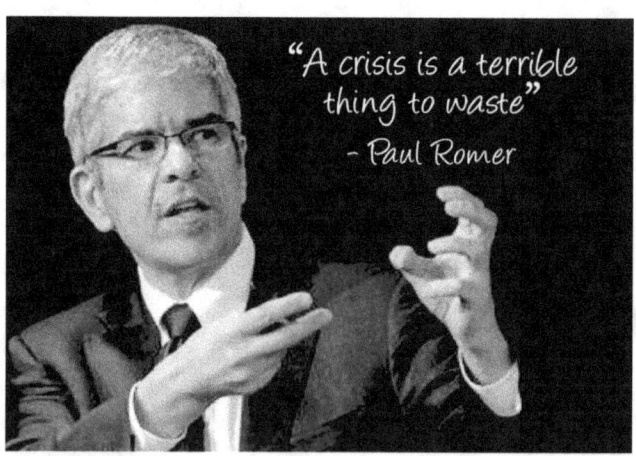

"A crisis is a terrible thing to waste"
– Paul Romer

From its heritage as a hospital products distribution company, the company remained oriented towards products in a market that had become more focused on services. At the same time, pressure from Wall Street pushed them from focusing on successful hospital system implementations to the financial performance of their product lines.

They recognized the need for research to update their understanding of how the buying center had changed, and what they needed to do to get back in. In particular, they wanted to understand the role of the IT director, who was not included in the company's standard set of clinical relationships.

FRESH INSIGHT

The findings were profound. In place of a few decision makers, there were now five, each from different disciplines, including an emerging new role (the Safety Officer) that was not so familiar to the company. The research into individual personas and how they interacted as a team:

- profiled all five **prospect personas** contributing to pump system decisions in the complex hospital environment,

- mapped their **team interaction** through the **purchase journey**,

- identified **targeted messages** for each persona from benefit ladders identifying the exact chain of features, benefits, and outcomes important to that persona, and

- translated those insights into a new **go-to-market strategy** that engaged each member of the consideration team.

They also identified the **Key Prospect Insight** for each role – the single most important truth to potentially connect them to each prospect.

They uncovered five powerful ways for they could **retake a leadership role** in the category, with clear tactics for accomplishing each goal.

LEARNING FROM OTHERS

Additionally, in the course of interviewing, they noticed a small **competitor** who was winning passionate fans for their implementation process. This emerged because they purposely profiled both prospects who they won and ones they lost.

Given the company's need to overcome serious product issues, it was understandable that they began with a focus on the **product.**

Nonetheless, the success of this small (but fast-growing) competitor provided compelling evidence for shifting focus to the system implementation **process** and the relationships developed by individual **people** in the implementation.

With the success of a competitor clearly portrayed, management decided to conduct more research to learn the specific strengths of this competitor's implementation process... and apply them for themselves.

A NEW DIRECTION

Thus armed, the marketing team was able to drive:

- **Messaging** that let them reconnect with each role in their own language and benefits, including IT and Quality/Risk Management roles, for the first time

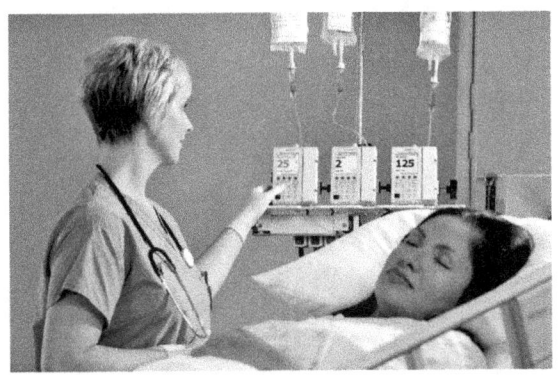

- **Positioning** to help redefine the market away from competitors and towards the new strengths they were bringing

- **Restructuring and staffing** of implementation teams

- A **unified vision** of the decision-making process/ buying center to engage and align other functional groups in the company, such as sales and support

- The development of a **new profit center**, based on the competitive implementation process.

Marketing management decided to take the competitive insights to heart and implement new staffing, new training, and a new onboarding process.

As a result, over the course of just four years, this company moved from **worst to first** in the industry-standard KLAS ratings for fusion pumps, powered largely by improvements in the implementation process.

About the Author

Wayne Cerullo founded B2P Partners to make B2B marketing more powerful by making it more personal. His passion is to help companies and individuals more effectively, and enjoyably serve the people who are their clients.

Wayne has helped shape the global marketing communications of IBM, Microsoft, and Intel while serving as planning director for their global agencies, Ogilvy & Mather, McCann-Erickson, and Euro RSCG. His work earned seven EFFIE awards for marketing effectiveness. Wayne also gained an appreciation for the client side of marketing at Citibank and EF Hutton.

Starting with a BA from Princeton University in the (oxymoronic) history of modernization, Wayne indulged his penchant for TLAs with an MBA from NYU. A former New Yorker and one-time Parisian, he currently lives in the San Francisco area with his wife, two children, and road bike.

PERSONA
Story 3

NEW WINE NEEDS
NEW SKINS

A story about market evolution,
competitive differentiation, and
a new market introduction for an
old-line company looking to enter
a new line of business.

Running a company successfully is always a challenge, even in good times. But when a company comes to the end of its normal growth cycle and needs to pivot into a new business – that's when the risks are highest and the resistance to change most palpable.

This is the story about a company every Baby Boomer remembers well – for a product few Millennials ever see. Back in the day, opening a checking account and getting your new (paper) checks was a rite of passage into adulthood. Deluxe checks were a part of life for many Americans.

With a sizeable chunk of the market and a product that cost pennies to make, profits were strong and predictable. Life at Deluxe Financial Services was good.

All that turned sour when technology and consumer behavior shifted inexorably from paper to plastic (credit and debit cards) and digital (bank bill payment services, wires, and eventually web-based transfers like PayPal and Venmo).

Deluxe saw this transition and decided to find and develop new ways to serve one of its core constituents, small businesses.

Deluxe Financial Products had recently acquired a long-established supplier of office products to small businesses. The newly merged company was anxious to explore options to increase growth within the current customer base, particularly in its top two vertical segments, but prior attempts to increase volume through new products and services or new marketing methods had borne minimal results. The client was looking to tap undiscovered or overlooked opportunities.

BETTER THINGS TO DO

A major challenge in gaining any insights within this sector was that their small business clients (wearing many hats) spent very little time thinking about this repetitive, low-involvement category. As a result, they realized they needed to use an observational (ethnographic) approach so they would learn what prospects really did rather than what they wanted to say they did. They all had better things to do other than think (and talk) about how they bought paper checks.

A THREE-STEP PLAN

1. Deluxe needed to get beyond a restatement of the problem (why customers don't buy more) to an

exploration of possible solutions (how and what they might buy) to potentially create new services and delivery modes that more closely reflected customers' and prospects' needs. The first step employed focus groups to stimulate discussion about buying criteria, desired vendor characteristics, and the competition.

2. As a second step, using the focus group information as a guide, the research team visited small business owners in their offices to observe how they worked, what they bought, and who they bought from. This fueled persona development, representing each vertical and mindset. These personas helped socialize the learning throughout the company and build momentum for the company's new direction.

3. Research then focused on generating insights into the prospect journey, building informed stories of how customers and prospects came to know about and purchase these products, yielding numerous insights about what it takes to win their attention and loyalty. Audio/video profiles were created so sponsoring internal clients could have a clear picture of their small business customers.

NEW OPPORTUNITIES

With these insights, Deluxe identified several new opportunities in this mature category. They outlined new product and service offerings, proposed new ways of segmenting customers to identify the highest-potential customers, ad identified new cross-channel sales and marketing strategies. Most importantly, they were also able to identify potential strategic partners.

Finally, Deluxe developed a "service platform" that would help drive a company-wide service culture, providing a key point of difference within this commodity market.

THE NEW DIRECTION

Persona research resulted in the development of a strategic partner acquisition team focused on strategic acquisitions that would expand their small business portfolio.

Findings also drove the creation of an SMB promotional group which supported and championed the success of their small business customers. The strategies and recommendations coming out of these insights has fueled a successful and expanded product and services offering as well as a strong strategic partnership and acquisition program.

About the Author

Dennis Flynn is an international marketing executive and author with over 25 years of experience in B2B and B2C sectors, having worked in various senior level positions in client-side, agency, and entrepreneurial environments.

After leading west coast offices for Saatchi & Saatchi and for BBDO, Dennis founded his own successful advertising agency serving international clients, including Toshiba and Gateway computers.

He then founded and ran a strategic consulting firm for several years, whose strategic planning model was adopted by Ericsson Mobile as a key part of their planning process. Summarizing lessons from his experience, Dennis then authored a book on branding titled Brand Clout.

On the corporate side, Dennis has built and led highly successful international business-focused and metrics-driven marketing teams for several mid-tier companies and enterprises.

With a BA and MBA from Adelphi University, Dennis has lived in New York, Chicago, and San Francisco, and now lives in Phoenix, AZ with his wife and two children.

PERSONA
Story 4

GOOD THING
WE CHECKED

A story about market expansion,
vertical marketing, and a new market
introduction for an energy technology
firm trying to enter a new sector.

WHAT'S OLD IS NEW AGAIN

For years, Excel Power (not their real name) has been the market leader of the supercapacitor market.

If you're wondering what supercapacitors are, therein lies part of the problem for a company and a technology that have been around since the mid-sixties.

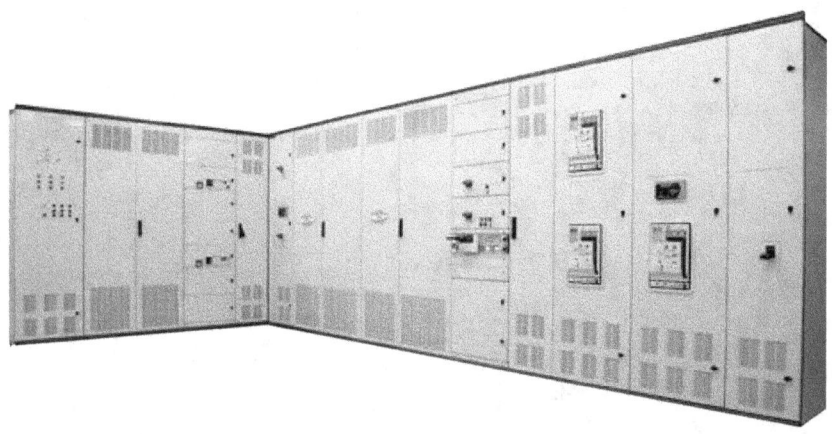

Despite the technology being around for so long, it is still "new" to many engineers, especially in contrast to batteries. And that is fortunate since, for much of the history of the company, offering "new and improved" technology was an effective sales strategy.

A supercapacitor is a power device similar to a battery. While batteries have low power and high energy capability, a supercapacitor has high power and low energy capability.

This is useful in applications that require quick, high bursts of energy for a short period of time. The added advantages of this technology over batteries are much faster recharging, much longer life, and better performance in high temperatures.

Applications where this is especially important include wind turbines (for controlling blade pitch), cars (for start/ stop), grid firming applications, industrial usage such as truck lifts, and onboard charging for hybrid buses. This story involves backup power in uninterruptible power supply (UPS) applications.

A NEEDED NEW MARKET

Excel Power had been enjoying success as the leader in a category that was seeing growth, in part as a result of the pressure on reducing CO_2 emissions and related growth in renewables and energy storage.

One of the markets identified as a potential growth market was the UPS market, which provides backup power for key installations such as data centers and hospitals. An extended loss in power within these segments can be financially devastating or life threatening.

It was within this market that an opportunity to position supercapacitors as a backup to batteries seemed viable. Pressure to succeed in this market was becoming especially strong as softness in other sectors created growing pressure to offset revenue losses.

UNINTENDED CONSEQUENCES

With excellent product characteristics vs. batteries in the UPS market, Excel Power started selling into this market as a "new and disruptive technology" to attract attention, build momentum, and highlight its advantages.

The company developed a penetration strategy that focused on selling into the top generator companies (Tier 1 firms) as a component sale. This would give them the chance to differentiate with the advantages of supercapacitors. Also, sales into just a few companies would cover a wide portion of the market. They would then be responsible for selling supercapacitors to the facility managers, who were the end-users. It was smart and efficient.

There was just one problem. It wasn't working.

TURN ON THE EMERGENCY LIGHTS

The intelligence provided by Excel Power's salesforce on this target market and its key target audience was proving ineffective and in some cases having a negative effect. The company needed to get a fresh, outside perspective on the decision makers and influencers in this business segment. The sales force supported any effort that would increase their success penetrating this new market.

In particular, Excel Power needed to gain more insight on the hospital or data center facility manager who selected this hardware. They needed to understand the full customer journey and the role of the solution provider in the consideration process.

A NEW LIGHT ON THE SUBJECT

The research included one-on-one discussions with the facility managers as end-users and the Tier 1 solution providers, as well as engineers and designers as influencers.

What was seemingly a proven, successful product-driven strategy in penetrating new markets proved not to be the case for this market.

The persona research revealed a very risk-adverse end-user who reacted negatively to any technology that was "new and disruptive". Using an intelligent positioning – one that was even obvious and proven – the company had nonetheless been selling **against** itself because it had not done the research with its personas from the start. They had been their own enemy.

The research also identified the Tier 1 solution provider as not wanting to introduce a solution incorporating a new technology to this risk-adverse audience.

Instead, they were looking to Excel Power to sell-in the technology to the end-user first, to be followed by the Tier 1 including it in their solution sell.

POWERING A NEW START

As a result of this learning, the product positioning was changed to one of a "long established, proven technology" that has been validated within numerous other applications.

Facility managers were encouraged to minimize their power risk by including supercapacitors as part of their diversified portfolio of backup technologies.

The new targeting and messaging strategies were used by marketing, and the salesforce saw **immediate success** in penetrating this market. The Marketing VP confirmed **higher response rates** to their marketing efforts using this strategy.

The Sales VP said, "*We didn't know what we didn't know,*" and confirmed the turn-around of their sales efforts were based on the insights and scripting provided by this research.

> *"It proved to be the insight we needed to tap into what is **now a lucrative market** for us."*

About the Author

Dennis Flynn is an international marketing executive and author with over 25 years of experience in B2B and B2C sectors, having worked in various senior level positions in client-side, agency, and entrepreneurial environments.

After leading west coast offices for Saatchi & Saatchi and for BBDO, Dennis founded his own successful advertising agency serving international clients, including Toshiba and Gateway computers.

He then founded and ran a strategic consulting firm for several years, whose strategic planning model was adopted by Ericsson Mobile as a key part of their planning process. Summarizing lessons from his experience, Dennis then authored a book on branding titled Brand Clout.

On the corporate side, Dennis has built and led highly successful international business-focused and metrics-driven marketing teams for several mid-tier companies and enterprises.

With a BA and MBA from Adelphi University, Dennis has lived in New York, Chicago, and San Francisco, and now lives in Phoenix, AZ with his wife and two children.

PERSONA
Story 5

THANK HEAVEN FOR
VERSION ELEVEN!

A story about increasing marketing effectiveness and accelerating the purchase cycle for an enterprise data security leader reaching out to the SMB market.

It was a dark and stormy meeting... at least for the marketing director at this large, well-known security software company. You see, this marketer was just given the assignment to launch the latest version of enterprise-level security software specifically designed for SMB (small & medium business).

Naturally, she and her team identified all the new features of Version 11 and highlighted how they would solve problems that Version 10 couldn't touch. And there were several.

Thank God for Version 11! The world was going to be a safer place! So now it was time to gear up for the launch...

MORE OF THE SAME

Except that incremental growth for new versions had pretty much stalled in recent years. And growth was needed for this flagship product! They considered doing a little checking with their persona to see how their messaging resonated before they

46

put the big bucks (and their reputations) behind it.

On the surface, this seemed like an **unnecessary diversion** of time and effort. This company had practically invented the category, they had been selling to SMB for years, and OMG this is Version ELEVEN!!

Seriously – what did they need to "figure out" about this? Why not just identify the top three new features and get going?!?

But... that's what the marketing managers for the previous versions had done, and results had not been stellar. As a result, it was decided to do a little persona research to find out how SMB decision makers actually made decisions about security software.

One dozen carefully-selected SMB prospects were interviewed in-depth about their purchase process, how they made choices among different products, and how data security fit into their business. This approach yielded lots of insights previously unknown from a relatively quick and inexpensive research effort. And they were glad they did start by understanding their prospects!

UP IS DOWN

First, they discovered that the **last thing** their prospects really wanted to know about was the **cool new features** of Version 11! These SMB business owners weren't in the market because of these new features – they just had an internal need for security software now.

Second, they were not excited about getting enterprise-level security for their SMB. In fact, they were **worried** that something that large and complex would **overwhelm** their small IT infrastructure. They wanted reassurance that software was small and efficient enough to let them operate as fast as usual. Less was more!

Finally, the more they heard about **features** they did not really understand – or want to understand – the more fear, uncertainty, and doubt (**FUD**) they felt. All they needed – or wanted – to know was that this software had been updated and optimized nearly a dozen times, so it was certainly good enough for them.

A MESSAGE PROSPECTS WANTED TO HEAR

In sum, the persona research revealed that the intended logical, even obvious, marketing strategy would have actually **suppressed** response!

In its place, a more persona-centric message was employed, promoting that this tested solution would **let small businesses keep humming** along smoothly.

And in response, marketplace response for version 11 was stronger than it was for the last several versions. All of this had the impact of greatly improving marketplace response ... and their careers!

About the Author

Wayne Cerullo founded B2P Partners to make B2B marketing more powerful by making it more personal. His passion is to help companies and individuals more effectively and enjoyably serve the people who are their clients.

Wayne has helped shape the global marketing communications of IBM, Microsoft, and Intel while serving as planning director for their global agencies, Ogilvy & Mather, McCann-Erickson, and Euro RSCG. His work earned seven EFFIE awards for marketing effectiveness. Wayne also gained an appreciation for the client side of marketing at Citibank and EF Hutton.

Starting with a BA from Princeton University in the (oxymoronic) history of modernization, Wayne indulged his penchant for TLAs with an MBA from NYU. A former New Yorker and one-time Parisian, he currently lives in the San Francisco area with his wife, two children, and road bike.

PERSONA
Story 6

DOING GOOD BY
DOING WELL

A story about increasing marketing effectiveness and shortening the purchase cycle for a small environmental consulting firm looking to win over the entire USA.

This is a story of a small group of environmental engineers (we'll call them ECO*) whose mission is to promote stewardship of the earth through water conservation. Specifically, they were dedicated to reducing water loss by helping the thousands of municipal water distribution systems around the country to identify and reduce their "Non-Revenue Water" (NRW).

NRW is an industry term for those millions of gallons of clean water that is collected but never does anyone good because it is lost to cracked pipes, faulty meters, or even theft. Every municipal water utility is losing water – the only question is whether it is in the single digits or as much as one-third of their total water capacity.

This "non-revenue water" costs us all hundreds of millions in financial and non-financial ways. It's a hidden disaster that impacts both the efficient usage of this finite resource, the people and industries that rely on it, and the revenue generation of the water utilities.

American Water Works Association

The starting point for all of this was to get an accurate, defensible audit of how much water each municipality was losing. No action could or would be taken until everyone knew and agreed on how much was being lost.

At the point this story begins, they had been doing this for two decades, primarily in the southeast US. It's important to note also that the entire global presence of ECO comprised a half-dozen engineers in one office.

CULTIVATING STEWARDSHIP OF OUR EARTHLY RESOURCES THROUGH INNOVATION.

The subhead above is more than their mission statement – stewardship through innovation – it is a guiding principal for ECO. They work together with their clients to effectively and cost-efficiently reduce waste and make smart infrastructure investments that support safe, sustainable supplies of water and energy for today and tomorrow.

And, for a relatively small team, they had big aspirations. Their target for growth for their next fiscal year was to more than double sales, which was their calculation of current staffing at full capacity. Meanwhile, they had competitors with literally hundreds of engineers, dozens of offices around the country, and national reputations.

Over their twenty years in existence, they had been through extreme boom and bust cycles. Ten years ago, they had 100 engineers and were growing like crazy, but when the bust cycle hit, they

had to let go of everyone and almost went out of business. They never, ever wanted to go through that again.

Their goal was to become as fully busy and profitable as they could without expanding. So that meant becoming much more effective... and efficient. And their current operation was far from efficient. They were cold-calling (and getting frost bitten), publishing a blog with little or no response, and spending too much time socializing over coffee during quiet times in the office.

They had to find a way to get prospects to reach out to them rather than fruitlessly knocking on thousands of municipal doors.

ONCE IN A LIFETIME OPPORTUNITY

The marketplace, at this moment in time, was presenting an enormous opportunity, because several states just decided to require their municipal utilities to complete a water loss audit and several states were experiencing prolonged drought conditions.

In addition, the National Water Works Industry Association (AWWA) decided to offer nationwide seminars on water loss auditing. With their experience and years of industry service, ECO was fortunate to be selected as the presenter. But how were they going to turn this high-time / low- fee training assignment into a flood (pun intended) of municipal consulting engagements?

GETTING A WHOLE LOT SMARTER

Working with an outside marketing group, a multi-step relationship development plan was outlined to nurture the larger, more profitable municipalities through several stages:

1. Identify the profile of the **top municipal targets** across the country.

2. Create awareness and establish the credentials of ECO as an **authority** in this hot field through AWWA teaching assignments.

3. Reinforce the **thought leadership** of ECO and engage prospects through more effective messaging on their website, blog, and presentation materials.

4. **Nurture prospects** from water audit training through to full engagements to implement water savings plans.

Efficiency was essential for this small firm to compete successfully with their limited resources. They could win only by working smarter. The objectives were smarter targeting, higher conversion rates, and shorter selling cycles.

To make this process as efficient as possible, and to find a new more effective way to engage large water utilities, it was decided to investigate the decision-making process at larger water utilities.

Two main persona roles were identified – water engineers and business managers – and their role throughout the decision-making process was identified.

This research process is based on in-depth conversations with a small number of carefully-selected prospects, here municipal water utility decision makers. The persona profiling research yields actionable insights regarding these executives as people with professional goals, needs, and interactive roles in the decision-making process.

CHOOSING WISELY

Instead of two, three personas emerged, with one being of particular importance. This was the one who will never do business with ECO, ever. Never. To paraphrase their comments:

> I don't have a problem. If I did
> have a problem, I don't need you to tell
> me about it. If I have a problem,
> I'm better able to solve it than you.

The two other personas represented the science and the business sides of the utility. The science persona ("water guy") was emotionally committed to stewardship – that water loss management was quite simply the right thing to do. The business persona was concerned with the economic impact of the lost revenue, and the cost and timing of recapturing it.

They, in turn, described their ideal partner in auditing and addressing their NRW situation, which was a blueprint for how ECO needed to be positioned. Perhaps of greatest importance, they, like Natty Bumppo (Hawkeye), guided ECO along their consideration path, pointing out areas of particular interest and concern which formed the basis of their new business push.

At capacity, and in reflection, a senior engineer at ECO said,

"The most important outcome to our business was being able to **shorten the time** *from initial handshake to contractual work. Usually, these NRW projects are big. They take a long time and a lot of money to complete, and they take a* **very long time to close**. *Ideas from our prospect research to* **accelerate that process** *have put us over the top. None of us have been in the office this week. We're all onsite with customers!"*

* Company name has been disguised

About the Author

International author, lecturer, and consultant, Scott Hornstein has worked with clients in all phases of marketing strategy, research, and implementation. His customer relationship methodology emphasizes respect and trust, and promotes opt-in relationships between marketers and their customers to maximize customer satisfaction, retention, and lifetime value.

He has worked with companies large and small to introduce and build new ideas to profitability, implement high-quality lead programs, improve marketing performance and accountability, and reengineer customer interfaces to boost satisfaction, referral, and return on investment.

B2B clients who have benefited from Scott's expertise include Microsoft, IBM, HP, AT&T, and Merrill Lynch, as well as Viryd Technologies, Applied Biosystems, Franklin Covey, and PaperDirect.

Scott's most recent book is Opt-In Marketing, and a second book will be coming out later this year. His articles and interviews have appeared in Brandweek, Adweek, Sales & Marketing Management, CRM, Catalog Age, BtoB, DMA Insider, The Toronto Star, and more. Scott's ability to make client companies hum reflects his own penchant for jazz, playing in an ensemble near his home base in Redding, CT.

www.ingramcontent.com/pod-product-compliance
Lightning Source LLC
Chambersburg PA
CBHW071236220526
45468CB00002B/881